Petroglyphs, Little Black Mountain, Arizona. Although it is nearly impossible to precisely date much rock art, clues such as the presence of lichens and the thickness of desert varnish on the pecked surface of petroglyphs lead experts to believe at least some rock art is centuries old. Some 500 designs have been catalogued at this site in northwest Arizona.

FROM THE ART on the ROCKS WISH YOU WERE HERE® POSTCARD BOOK

SIERRA PRESS, INC. , PO BOX 430, EL PORTAL, CA 95318

Three Rivers Petroglyph Site, New Mexico. This site, near Carrizozo, New Mexico, is situated atop a low rock outcrop in the Tularosa Basin. Nearly 20,000 glyphs have been catalogued here. The Jornado Mogollon culture responsible for all this art probably enjoyed the view of 12,000-foot Sierra Blanca, lying a few miles to the east.

FROM THE ART on the ROCKS WISH YOU WERE HERE® POSTCARD BOOK

SIERRA PRESS, INC. , PO BOX 430, EL PORTAL, CA 95318

PHOTO: © JEFF NICHOLAS

San Rafael Swell, Utah. The "Rainbow Panel", shown here, was probably created by the Fremont people who inhabited this region prior to A.D.1300. While the Fremonts left little in the way of artifacts of their material culture, they did leave a wealth of rock art. Its significance, like most rock art, can only be guessed at by modern researchers.

FROM THE ART on the ROCKS WISH YOU WERE HERE® POSTCARD BOOK

SIERRA PRESS, INC. , PO BOX 430, EL PORTAL, CA 95318

PHOTO: © TOM TILL

Hopi Clan Rocks, Near Tuba City, Arizona. The Hopi Salt Trail, which is still in use today, is lined with rocks and boulders decorated with the clan symbols of the Hopi. Generations, on pilgrimages to the Little Colorado River, have left their marks - corn plants, Kachinas, sun figures, birds, snakes, lizards and much more.

FROM THE ART on the ROCKS WISH YOU WERE HERE® POSTCARD BOOK

SIERRA PRESS, INC. , PO BOX 430, EL PORTAL, CA 95318

PHOTO: © BRUCE HUCKO

Great Gallery, Canyonlands N.P., Utah. One of the most famous panels of rock art in the southwest, these ghostly figures are older than either the Fremont or Anasazi rock art found in the same area. These larger than life-size pictographs are representative of the Barrier Canyon Style, which consists of both petroglyphs and pictographs.

FROM THE ART on the ROCKS WISH YOU WERE HERE® POSTCARD BOOK

SIERRA PRESS, INC., PO BOX 430, EL PORTAL, CA 95318

PHOTO: © DIANA STRATTON

Kokopelli, Rio Grande Valley, New Mexico. Named after the contemporary Pueblo Kachina, to whom he bears a resemblance, Kokopelli is one of the most enduring figures in southwestern rock art. Variously interpreted as a Rain Priest, Hunting Magician or Fertility Figure, this humpbacked flute player is seen in numerous places where Anasazi rock art is found.

FROM THE ART on the ROCKS WISH YOU WERE HERE® POSTCARD BOOK

SIERRA PRESS, INC., PO BOX 430, EL PORTAL, CA 95318

Hand Prints, Indian Creek, Utah. These handprints, a very popular design motif, are in a rock alcove near Newspaper Rock State Park in southeast Utah. The "negative" effect was achieved by blowing paint through a hollow reed around the hand which was held against the stone surface.

FROM THE ART on the ROCKS WISH YOU WERE HERE® POSTCARD BOOK

SIERRA PRESS, INC. , PO BOX 430, EL PORTAL, CA 95318

PHOTO: © FRED HIRSCHMANN

Petrified Forest N.P., Arizona. This man/lizard is one of literally hundreds of Anasazi petroglyphs found around the bluff that Puerco Ruin is built upon. The crumbling edge of this bluff provided countless dark stone faces upon which rock artists pecked their designs; masked figures, geometric patterns and animal figures abound.

FROM THE ART on the ROCKS WISH YOU WERE HERE® POSTCARD BOOK

SIERRA PRESS, INC. , PO BOX 430, EL PORTAL, CA 95318

PHOTO: © JEFF NICHOLAS

Capitol Reef N.P., Utah. The cliffs and boulders along the Fremont River are the location of dozens of anthropomorphic figures created by the Fremont culture. These figures, done in the Southern San Rafael Style, were typically outfitted in exotic ornamentation; earrings, necklaces, belts and elaborate headdresses are common.

FROM THE ART on the ROCKS WISH YOU WERE HERE® POSTCARD BOOK

SIERRA PRESS, INC. , PO BOX 430, EL PORTAL, CA 95318

PHOTO: © MARY ALLEN

Petrified Forest N.P., Arizona. Within this park are thousands of petroglyphs pecked into stone. A number of sites, such as this one in the backcountry, display astonishing "Newspaper Rocks" where entire stone faces are decorated with a wide range of subjects. While animal motifs are very common, human figures, masks and geometric patterns are also regularly encountered.

FROM THE ART on the ROCKS WISH YOU WERE HERE® POSTCARD BOOK

SIERRA PRESS, INC. , PO BOX 430, EL PORTAL, CA 95318

PHOTO: © FRED HIRSCHMANN

Canyonlands N.P., Utah. There are several alcoves in the canyons south of the Needles District where remarkably abstracted pictographs such as these can be found. Because of the resemblance between faces depicted in rock art and Fremont clay figurines, archaeologists believe the faces motif may have been painted by Fremont, rather than the Anasazi known to inhabit the area.

FROM THE ART on the ROCKS WISH YOU WERE HERE® POSTCARD BOOK

SIERRA PRESS, INC. , PO BOX 430, EL PORTAL, CA 95318

PHOTO: © RANDALL K. ROBERTS

Newspaper Rock State Park, Utah. Situated near the cool green banks of Indian Creek in southeast Utah, "Newspaper Rock" displays a staggering variety of subjects, styles and ages. Design motifs include circles, humans, animals, even figures mounted on horseback are recorded here, each painstakingly pecked into the dark stone surface.

FROM THE ART on the ROCKS WISH YOU WERE HERE® POSTCARD BOOK

SIERRA PRESS, INC. , PO BOX 430, EL PORTAL, CA 95318

PHOTO: © JIM WILSON

Saguaro N. M., Arizona. Situated atop a low rock outcrop in the western portion of the park, these figures beckon to the visitor with their mysterious beauty. Hohokam people, working in the Gila Petroglyph style, pecked these meticulous designs on suitable surfaces scattered across southern Arizona. Picture Rocks State Park near Gila Bend is another excellent site of similar rock art.

FROM THE ART on the ROCKS WISH YOU WERE HERE® POSTCARD BOOK

SIERRA PRESS, INC. , PO BOX 430, EL PORTAL, CA 95318

PHOTO: © JIM WILSON

Chaco Culture N.H.P., New Mexico. One of the most perplexing aspects of rock art is the inability for most of us to know for certain what they mean. This panel, near Peñasco Blanco, is significant because it is believed to represent the supernova witnessed on Earth in A.D.1054. This awareness and knowledge of the sky is consistent with what we know of the Chacoan Anasazi, who constructed numerous "calendars" to record both Summer and Winter solstices, most likely for agricultural purposes.

FROM THE ART on the ROCKS WISH YOU WERE HERE® POSTCARD BOOK

SIERRA PRESS, INC. , PO BOX 430, EL PORTAL, CA 95318